You can colour all the black and white pictures.

This is Peter.   Here they are.

This is Peter.   Here they are.

This is Jane.

This is Jane.

This is Peter.
This is Jane.
This is a dog.
They are here.

This is Pat.

This is Pat

T

Pat is a dog.
They like the dog.

The

Pat

The dog has a ball.
Here is a toy dog.
Pat plays with Peter.
Pat is in a shop.

Here

Pat

 fun in the water

fun in the water

f

Here they are in the water.
They have fun in the water.

Jump in, says Jane to Peter.
It is fun, Peter says.
They look at Pat.
Jane plays with water.

It..

....

....

....

....

....

....

....

Look at this fish.

Look at this fish.

L

Jane says, Look at this.
Peter, have a look.

ball,   a fish,   Jane,   some trees,
ome water,   Peter,   Pat,   some toys

1_______________________

2_______________________

3_______________________

4_______________________

1_______________________

2_______________________

3_______________________

4_______________________

Have a go, he say

Have a go, he say

H

Jane wants to have a go.
Here I come, she says.

rite the sentences correctly, by the pictures.

Jane says, Yes, I want it.
Peter has a go.
Have some sweets, he says.
They like to look.

some for you

some for you

s

Here are some
for you, Jane,
and some for you, Peter.

water. He into jumps the

He jumps ....

dogs. the at Look

....

Jane No, says, no.

....

go home. They

....

Write the words.   We like to shop.
We like to shop.
W

They have to go to the shops.
We can go in here, says Jane.
Yes, we like to shop in here,
says Peter.

Look in here, Jane says.
They like to jump.
He is in the tree.
Peter has a go.

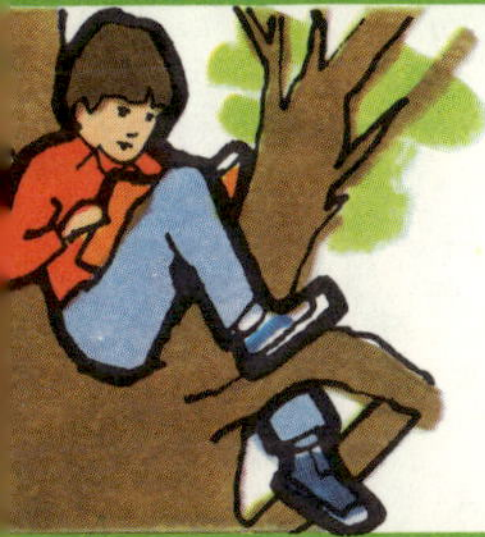

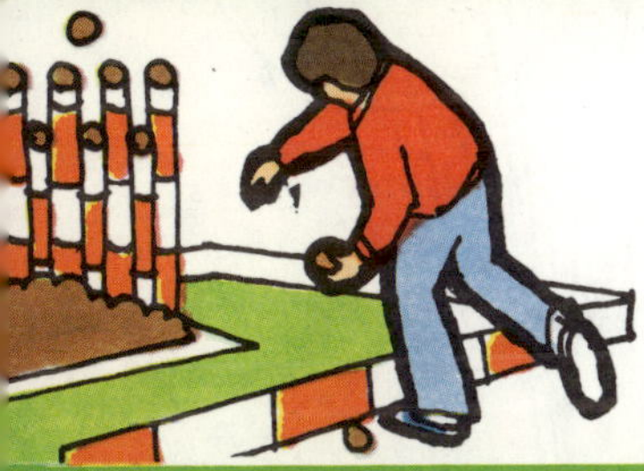

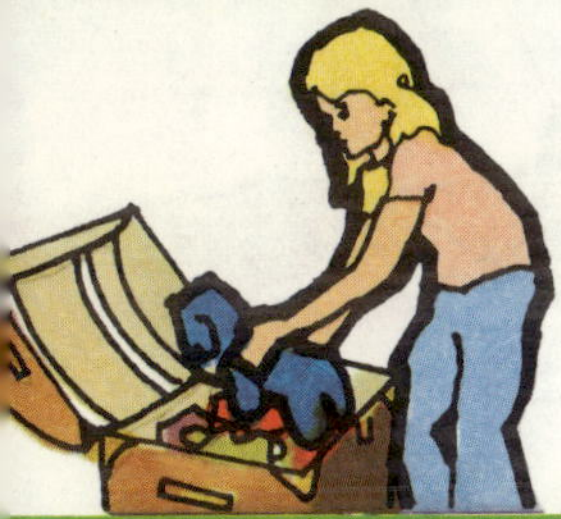

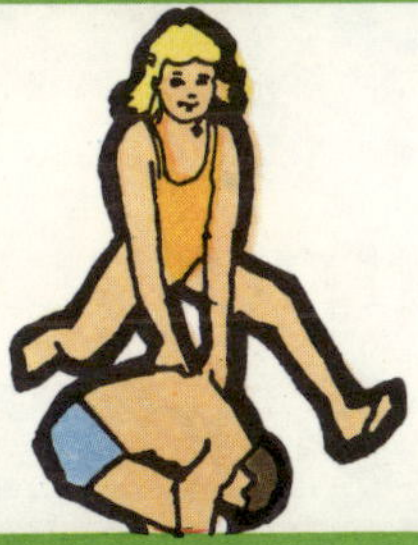

They can jump.

They can jump.

T

Peter has a ....
(for, fish, fun)

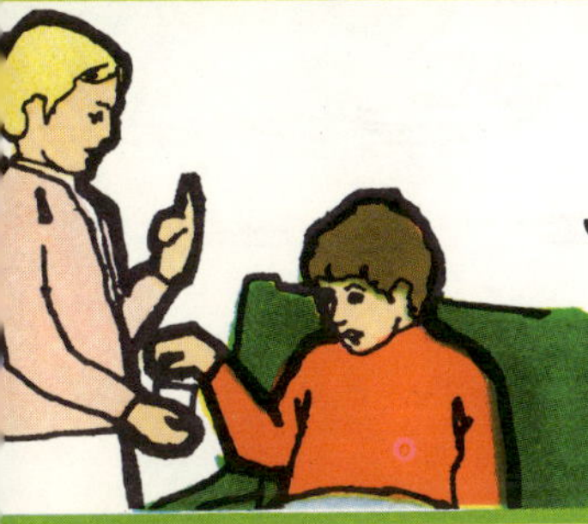

Jane has some ....
(shop, says, sweets)

The dog has a ....
(fish, ball, tree)

He likes to ....
(with, wants, write)

They have some ....
(trees, toy, toys)

Come here, he says

Come here, he says

c

Look at Pat, says Jane.
You come here, says Peter.
Pat, Pat, come here.

rite the sentences correctly, by the pictures.

1 They like to play. They have fun.
2 Come, come, he says to the dog.
3 Here it is. I have it, he says.
4 Look at this, Jane says.

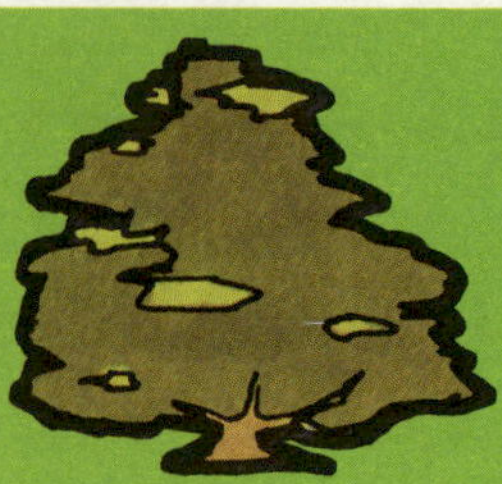

Is it a tree?

.......Ye

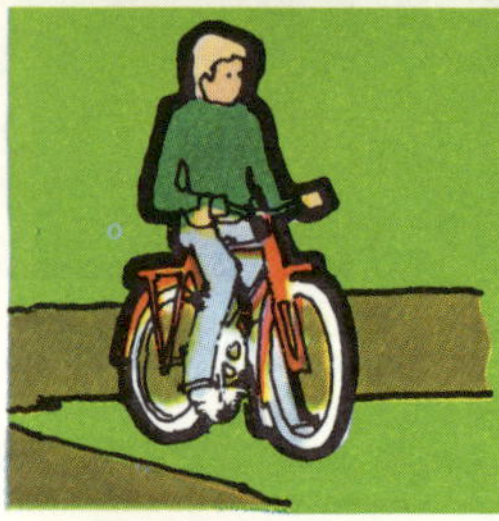

Is he in water?

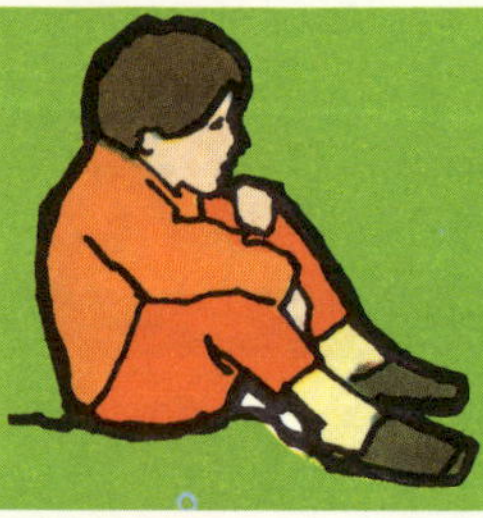

....

Is this a dog?

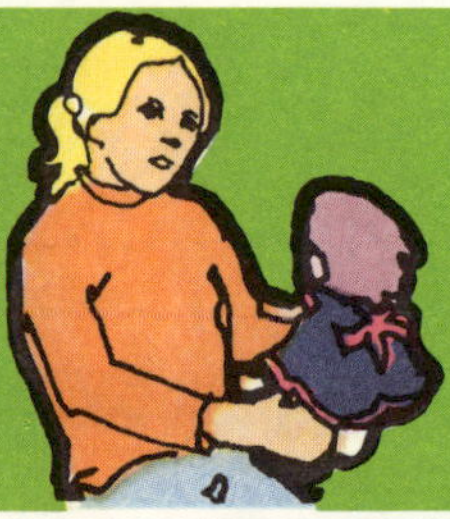

....

Has Jane a toy?

....

Are they in a shop?

....

Has the dog a ball?

....

They like to look
at toys.
It wants the fish.
This is fun, he says.
They are in a tree.

dog, shop, sweets, read,
write, fish, tree, jumps

1 Pat is a _ _ _.

2 They go to a _ _ _ _
for some _ _ _ _ _ _.

3 Peter and Jane can
_ _ _ _ and _ _ _ _ _.

4 Here is a _ _ _ _.

5 Look at this _ _ _ _.

6 He _ _ _ _ _ into
the water.

It can jump ....

They can jump ....

He has ....

Peter looks ....

Jane wants ....

They like to ....

Jane can jump.
They are at home.
Jane reads and Peter play
Here is some for you.

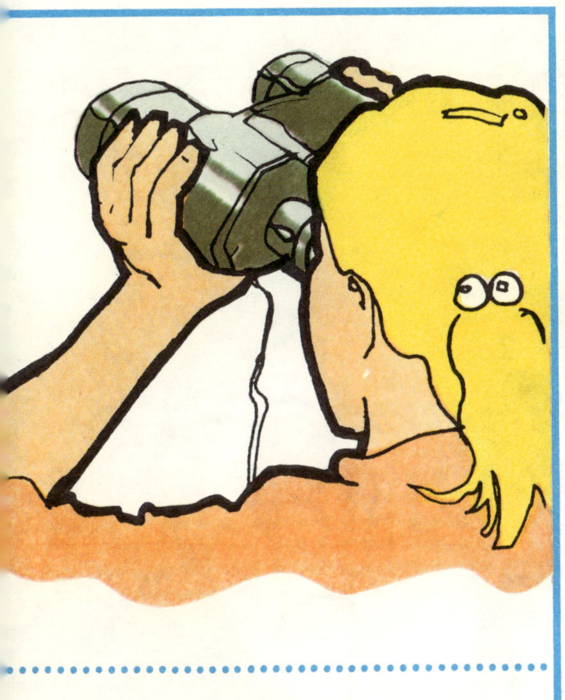

He has to jump.
Jane has a look.
They have fun
with the fish.
He has fun
with the dog.

Write a number in each circle to match
the pictures below.

◯ Jane reads.　　　　◯ Peter writes.

◯ It is for you, Jane says.　　　◯ Peter reads.

◯ It is for you, he says.　　　◯ Jane writes.

Can you read?   ....

Can you write?   ....

Are you Peter?   ....

Are you Jane?   ....

Have you a dog?   ....

Have you a home?   ....

Are you in a shop?   ....

Are you at home?   ....

Are you at play?   ....if correct

Can you jump?   ....

This   this   Pat   they   They

are   Are   water   fun   it

It   says   have   Have   he   He

look   fish   wants   no   Some

some   for   you   You   can   Can

jump   jumps   Jump   into   We

we   go   sweets   home   Come

come